SPARKLE

The ABC of Smarter Living

NKECHI L. IFEDIORA

Copyright © 2024 by Nkechi L. Ifediora

All rights reserved. No part of this publication may be reproduced, distributed, or transmitted in any form or by any means, including photocopying, recording, or other electronic or mechanical methods, without the publisher's prior written permission, except for brief quotations embodied in critical reviews and specific other non-commercial uses permitted by copyright law.

For permission requests, email addressed "Attention: Permissions Coordinator" at:hello@worthwriting.co.uk

Publisher: Independently published
Book Editing and Design by Worth Writing
www.worthwriting.co.uk

ISBN
Paperback: 978-1-0686435-0-7
Hardback: 978-1-0686435-1-4

Printed in the United Kingdom.

Dedication

This book is dedicated to my father, Dr Cyril Ogbonnaya Joseph, 'COJ'—the ultimate 'girl dad'! He was unapologetically devoted to supporting his daughters. I love you, Dad. Continue to rest in peace.

Acknowledgement

I extend my deepest gratitude to the Lord Jesus, whose guidance and presence have been a constant source of strength and inspiration throughout my journey. My faith remains integral to my identity, shaping every aspect of my life.

I am forever indebted to my parents, whose unwavering love, support, and guidance have played a pivotal role in shaping the person I am today. Though they are no longer with us, their legacy lives on in my heart, and I am eternally grateful for the values they instilled in me.

To my beloved husband and children, your unwavering support, love, and encouragement have been the cornerstone of my success. Your belief in me has fuelled my determination and perseverance, and I am immensely grateful for the sacrifices you have made along the way. Without you, this book would not have been possible.

I also want to express my heartfelt appreciation to my publishers, Worth Writing, for believing in me and providing the platform to share my insights and experiences with the world. Your dedication and commitment to excellence have helped this book shine.

With profound gratitude,
Nkechi
London, April 2024

Contents

Introduction 1
  Unlocking the Smarter Life 1
  My story 3
  Your sparkle begins today. 4

Chapter 1: The Power of Smart Living 8
  Why it matters 8
  Managing the personal in the professional world 9
  A sneak peek into smart living 12

Chapter 2: Cracking the Code 15
  The ABCD of Smart Living 15
  Accept and assess: embracing reality and identifying opportunities 16
  Boundaries and values: defining your non-negotiables and core beliefs 17
  Community: assemble your tribe 18
  Decision: empowerment through strategic choices ... 19

Chapter 3: Acceptance and Assessment 22
  Mastering the Art 22
  Establishing your baseline 24
  Empowering actions: applying acceptance and assessment 31

Chapter 4: Boundaries for Smart Living 33

Setting the stage 33
Being clear about our values 35
Taking action towards smart living 37

Chapter 5: Thriving Together 39
Leveraging the strength of your community 39
Taking action towards community thriving 44

Chapter 6: Decision Making 46
Mastering the art of Making the Call 46

Chapter 7: Sparkle Enablers 49
Leadership 51
Smart technology 54
Mindfulness 56
Emotional intelligence 58
Self-care and glow-up plans 61

Chapter 8: GLOW UP! 64
Glow-up essentials 64

Chapter 9: EPILOGUE – SPARKLING 86

References 88

Introduction

Unlocking the Smarter Life

Over the last 30 years, I have worked in highly-pressured leadership roles, sometimes in adverse environments; raised my three children; studied and led research; nurtured my marriage; run a house; advised and led work for a range of charities; and been part of a strong and supportive network of friends and family.

Let me be clear: I am not a Superwoman. But I have learned some key things and want to share them.

My generation of women was told we could have it all. My experience has shown me that this is true—so long as we don't try to do it all. We must be smart about what we do, what we outsource, and how we prioritise. That is the way to achieve a life with sparkle.

My professional journey as an executive director within the complex healthcare sector has involved everything from massively increasing access to therapy for people in distress to overseeing the rollout of lifesaving care, particularly to highly vulnerable communities. It has been and continues to be enriching and demanding.

Sparkle

But let's be honest: life as a mother, a wife, and a leader often catches one off guard. It's woven with moments of triumph and challenge, and balance can feel elusive.

You may have found yourself drawn to this book in search of answers. I want to help you increase your effectiveness amidst life's complexities. I'm here to inspire and guide you towards a more fulfilling existence.

So, let us embark together on this voyage, unravelling the mysteries of smarter living and charting a course towards a life with sparkle.

With love and sparkles,
Nkechi

My story

On a cold and windy weekend in 2007, I was in a situation many of you may have experienced. I had a demanding job, three wonderful children, and numerous domestic responsibilities, all while studying my dream course. My babysitter had just cancelled, and I needed to attend my course that Saturday to complete the programme. This was my last chance, and I had to decide quickly. I decided to bring my children with me to central London, and thankfully, everything worked out. After returning home, I made a list of my weekly activities and decided to start living smarter. That was when the seeds for this book began to grow.

As a working mother, I've had my fair share of challenges finding the 'secret sauce' that helps me balance and prioritise effectively. It has been a constant process of trial and error, a delicate dance between my career, family, and personal life. As ambitious professionals striving to excel in both our personal and professional spheres, we have just 24 hours a day (sometimes, it feels like even less), and there's always a list of things vying for our time and attention.

One of the most valuable lessons I learned from my dad was about the importance of time. 'Is that the best use of your time?' he would ask. Time is a precious commodity, one we can't control. In this complex, multifaceted world, we must prioritise effectively. If something is better done by someone else, then so be it! This allows us to play to our strengths, focus on what we enjoy, and add value to them. However, it's not sustainable to pile all those things on one person – whether you or anyone else. There needs to be a network of contacts/people/friends you can link with, depending on your needs.

Getting this right is not just a quick fix; it's an empowerment tool. It's about ensuring that you and your relationships are more rounded and have more quality time for the people and things you love. This book doesn't just offer advice; it presents a four-step approach to strategically outsourcing and helping you live smarter… helping you sparkle!

Your sparkle begins today.

As defined by the Cambridge dictionary, strategic outsourcing involves entrusting specific tasks to external entities for greater efficiency or cost-effectiveness. In this book, I explore the notion of 'outsourcing' or 'sharing' facets of our personal lives to enhance value and improve our effectiveness. In this digital age, the array of available tools makes such practices more accessible. From task management apps to online marketplaces for services, we have many options to make us more effective, giving us time to sparkle.

What do I mean by 'outsourcing/sharing'? 'Sharing' could be as simple as inviting a friend to watch a movie, while 'outsourcing' might involve asking a friend to book the tickets for you. The critical difference is that 'sharing' involves mutual participation, while 'outsourcing' implies delegating a task to someone else. Ultimately, these strategic decisions empower us to live smarter, fostering efficiency and enriching our quality of life.

In the corporate realm, outsourcing has become commonplace, with companies making the most of external expertise to streamline operations and maximise productivity. Businesses can focus on growth and innovation by reallocating time-consuming tasks or functions to specialised partners, driving profitability.

Consider the possibilities: what could you achieve with an extra three hours each day if you freed yourself from mundane tasks like grocery shopping, laundry, or cleaning?

You could dedicate more time to refining that business plan and pursuing your entrepreneurial dreams with renewed vigour. Or you could prioritise self-care, improving your physical and mental well-being with regular exercise. And let's not forget the importance of quality time spent with loved ones — a precious commodity in the hustle and bustle of modern life.

As you delve into the pages of this book, I invite you to reconsider your relationships and connections through a lens of mutual value creation. The fundamental principle of strategic outsourcing is to create value for both parties involved. Applying this principle to your relationships ensures that you and the other person benefit from the interaction. My aim is to help you survive and empower you to thrive, unlocking the full potential of your personal and professional relationships. Let today mark the beginning of your journey toward a brighter, more fulfilling existence.

A crucial part of what I will share with you is the ABCD framework I have devised and developed, which underpins the approach I set out in this book.

Introducing the ABCD concept:

- **Accept and assess:** First, you embrace your current circumstances while objectively evaluating areas for improvement, fostering a mindset of self-awareness and growth.
- **Boundaries and values:** Defining your personal boundaries and core values empowers you to make decisions aligned with your authentic selves and overarching life goals.
- **Community:** Exploring the significance of cultivating meaningful connections and nurturing supportive networks helps you to recognise the collective strength and enrichment that community brings to your life.
- **Decision:** You will master the art of decision-making with clarity and confidence, using the

insights you have gained from acceptance, boundary-setting, and understanding the strength of your communities.

The ABCD concept is your guide, providing a structured approach to propel you towards informed and purposeful choices. It will ensure you feel guided and supported on your growth journey.

Chapter 1
The Power of Smart Living

Why it matters

In the hustle and bustle of modern life, smart living is more than just a passing trend — it's crucial for thriving in a fast-paced world. But why does it matter? Why should we prioritise purposeful choices and strategic actions in our daily lives?

The answer is that it can profoundly impact our overall well-being and success. By adopting a mindset of conscious living and making informed decisions about our health, relationships, and goals, we empower ourselves to navigate life's complexities with clarity and purpose.

Scientific and physiological research underscores the far-reaching benefits of smart living. Studies reveal that strategic lifestyle choices can optimise our brains and minds, strengthen our emotional resilience, and reduce our risk of chronic diseases. From how we eat and exercise to how we manage stress and cultivate relationships, every aspect of our lives plays a crucial role in shaping our long-term health and happiness.

Moreover, smart living extends beyond individual benefits for each of us to benefits for society as a whole. We contribute to our communities' collective health and prosperity by prioritising personal well-being and sustainable living. From reducing healthcare costs to fostering economic productivity, the ripple effects of smart living reverberate far and wide.

In essence, the pursuit of smart living is not just about getting the most from our lives—it's about building a brighter, more resilient future for ourselves and future generations. By embracing the power of purposeful choices and strategic actions, we unlock our full potential and pave the way for a world defined by vitality, purpose, and fulfilment.

Managing the personal in the professional world

As we step into our workplaces or embark on our entrepreneurial endeavours each day, it's essential to recognise that we don't shed our identities at the door. On the contrary, our personal lives intertwine with our professional pursuits, shaping whether and how far we can be our best selves. This dynamic interplay is vividly depicted in the 'wheel of life[1],' a holistic tool that offers a

---

[1] The Wheel of Life... ∗ BRILLIANCE WITHIN

Sparkle

panoramic view of our existence and guides us towards achieving balance across its many elements.

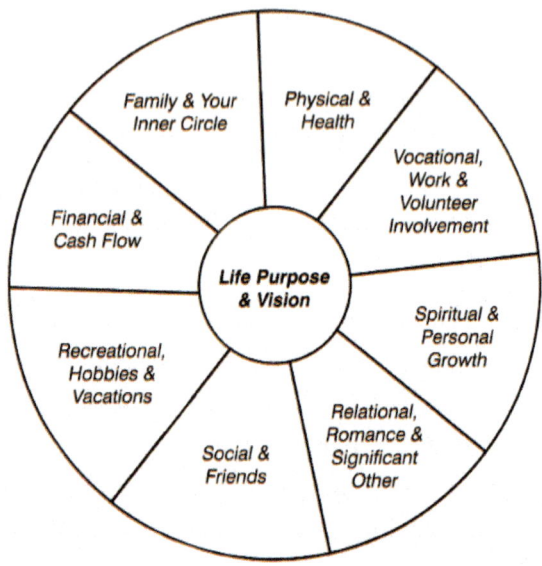

Our lives span many areas that determine our overall satisfaction and success, from family relationships to physical well-being, financial stability, and work passions. I have developed the '7 Ls' below to define these vital aspects of our existence.

- Live: health, vitality, and our aspirations for personal fulfilment.
- Love: the depth of our relationships and sense of belonging.

- Learn: about our ongoing personal growth and development.
- Laugh: leisure, recreation, and joy in our lives.
- Lead: the impact and influence we have in our chosen fields.
- La Monnaie: our finances and financial choices.
- Legacy: the impact we leave behind us that transcends generations.

We must acknowledge that we need help to truly excel in these different elements. We need a dedicated team's support, a nurturing community's guidance, and the humility to recognise our limitations. This is where strategic outsourcing in our personal lives is so important—the planned delegation of tasks and responsibilities that affords us the time and space to focus on what truly matters.

For many of us, the onset of the COVID-19 pandemic and the subsequent adoption of remote work arrangements blurred the boundaries between our professional and personal lives like never before. In this ever-connected world, we often face the challenge of simultaneously managing the personal and professional spheres. Whether we're navigating virtual meetings from our kitchen tables or juggling childcare responsibilities alongside conference calls, the spotlight of our professional identities shines brightly—almost incessantly.

Where the lines between work and life blur, it's imperative that we cultivate resilience, embrace flexibility, and prioritise self-care. By navigating this delicate balancing act thoughtfully and gracefully, we will safeguard our well-being and unlock the full potential of our professional endeavours and personal aspirations.

A sneak peek into smart living

Before we explore smart living and how it works, I thought I'd quickly equip you with practical strategies and actionable techniques to empower you to navigate life's complexities confidently and purposefully. For ambitious professionals striving to excel in both their personal and professional spheres, mastering the art of smart living is not just a luxury—it's a requirement for success.

1. Time management mastery: Time is our most precious resource, and using it well is critical to achieving our full potential. Explore techniques such as time blocking, prioritisation, and task batching to maximise productivity and minimise stress. By embracing a proactive approach to time management, you can carve out dedicated time for both work and personal pursuits, ensuring a harmonious balance between the two.

2. Stress reduction strategies: In today's fast-paced world, stress has become an unavoidable companion on our journey towards success. How we manage stress will determine whether or not we thrive. Explore stress reduction techniques such as mindfulness meditation, deep breathing exercises, and regular physical activity. By incorporating these practices into your daily routine, you can cultivate resilience and maintain a sense of calm amidst life's inevitable challenges.

3. Prioritisation principles: With competing demands vying for our attention, prioritising effectively is paramount. Embrace the Pareto Principle (the 80/20 rule) to identify the tasks and activities that yield the most significant impact and focus your energy accordingly. Additionally, use tools such as Eisenhower's Urgent/Important matrix to categorise tasks based on their urgency and importance, allowing you to allocate resources wisely and achieve optimal outcomes.

4. Work-life integration: Rather than striving for an elusive work-life balance, embrace the concept of work-life integration — a seamless blending of professional responsibilities and personal pursuits. Explore strategies for setting boundaries, establishing designated 'no-work' zones, and fostering open communication with colleagues

Sparkle

and loved ones. You can experience greater fulfilment and satisfaction in both realms by cultivating a holistic approach to life.

5. Setting SMART Goals: Goal-setting is the cornerstone of smart living. It provides a roadmap for success, guiding our actions towards tangible outcomes. Embrace the SMART criteria — Specific, Measurable, Achievable, Relevant, and Time-bound — to craft clear, actionable goals that align with your values and aspirations. SMART goals can harness the power of purpose to help you make meaningful progress towards achieving your personal and professional dreams.

It is essential to remember that smart living is not about perfection but progress. Embrace these strategies with an open mind and a willingness to adapt, knowing that each small step forward brings you closer to the vibrant, fulfilling life you deserve.

Chapter 2
Cracking the Code

The ABCD of Smart Living

We often face a labyrinth of choices and complexities in our quest for smart living. We need a map to help us navigate the terrain with confidence and clarity. Enter the ABCD of smart living—an innovative framework designed to crack the code of intentional living and empower ambitious professionals to thrive in every aspect of our lives.

The ABCD framework has four elements: acceptance and assessment, boundaries and values, community, and decision. Together, they enable a consistent, systematic approach to transforming our lofty aspirations into tangible realities. Armed with the ABCD, we can embark on a journey of self-discovery and empowerment with the tools and insights needed to chart a course towards fulfilment and success.

Accept and assess: embracing reality and identifying opportunities

This initial phase sets the stage for success, challenging us to embrace our humanity and confront the realities of our current lifestyle. We lay a foundation for intentional living and strategic action by accepting our limitations and assessing our priorities.

Accept: The first step towards smart living is acknowledging a fundamental truth — we are not superwomen. In a world that glorifies hustle culture and perpetual productivity, it's easy to fall into the trap of believing that we must do it all. However, true wisdom lies in recognising our limitations and embracing a mindset of self-compassion and authenticity.

Assess: With acceptance comes the opportunity for assessment — an introspective journey that illuminates how we allocate our most precious resource: time. Take stock of your daily routines, obligations, and commitments. Reflect on the value of your time and consider what truly brings you joy and fulfilment. Identify the tasks and responsibilities that energise you and those that drain your resources. You lay the groundwork for intentional living and strategic decision-making by clarifying your priorities and preferences.

Boundaries and values: defining your non-negotiables and core beliefs

Establishing clear boundaries and aligning our actions with our core values is essential in pursuing smart living. This phase of the ABCD framework challenges us to delve deep into our psyches, identifying our non-negotiables and clarifying our fundamental beliefs, creating space for authenticity and fulfilment in every aspect of our lives.

What are your no-go areas? As we navigate the complexities of life, it's essential to recognise and honour our boundaries — those areas of life where compromise is not an option. Reflect on the aspects of your existence that bring you discomfort or conflict, whether sacrificing your well-being for the sake of others, tolerating toxic relationships, or neglecting your passions and desires. By delineating your no-go areas, you reclaim agency over your life and establish a framework for healthy boundaries.

What are your beliefs? At the core of every individual lies a set of deeply held beliefs — guiding principles that shape our perceptions, decisions, and actions. Take time to explore your values, considering the ideals and convictions that resonate most deeply with your authentic self. Whether it's integrity, compassion, creativity, or justice, your beliefs serve as the compass that guides you through the myriad challenges and opportunities of life. By embracing your beliefs with unwavering conviction, you cultivate a sense of purpose and authenticity that fuels your journey towards smart living.

Community: assemble your tribe

Smart living is not a solitary endeavour — it thrives within the context of supportive communities and informed decisions. A strong community is essential to reap the full benefits of smart living. It gives us the necessary support, guidance, and connections to thrive. This crucial phase of the ABCD framework invites you to assemble your tribe — a diverse network of friends, family, contacts and acquaintances who enrich your life and empower you to thrive.

Friends and family: At the heart of every strong community lies the bond of friendship and family — a web of relationships that nourishes our souls and sustains us through the trials and triumphs of life. Invest in cultivating deep, meaningful connections with those closest to you, prioritising quality time and open communication. Lean on your friends and family for support, guidance, and encouragement in the knowledge that you are a source of strength and solace for them, just as they are for you.

Contacts and neighbours: Beyond the confines of our immediate social circle lies a vast network of contacts and neighbours — individuals whose paths intersect with ours in myriad ways. Whether it's the fellow parent at your child's school, the local business owner, or the neighbour next door, these connections offer many opportunities for collaboration, support, and community building. Take time to nurture these relationships, reaching out with genuine curiosity and a spirit of generosity. You will create a support system extending beyond your immediate social circle by fostering a sense of interconnectedness within your local community.

Acquaintances: Another group is the vast array of people we encounter daily, from colleagues and classmates to fellow commuters. While these connections may seem superficial, they possess much potential for mutual support and collaboration. Create meaningful interactions with acquaintances, fostering genuine connections that transcend surface-level interactions. You never know when they may be a source of invaluable insights or unexpected opportunities.

Decision: empowerment through strategic choices

This pivotal phase of the ABCD framework challenges us to make decisions with intentionality and purpose, guided by a deep understanding of our values and aspirations so that we prioritise what truly matters.

Decide: At the heart of smart living lies the art of decision-making — deliberate choices that steer our lives towards fulfilment and success. As you embark on your smart living journey, assess what aspects of your life you can outsource or share to optimise efficiency and enhance quality.

Consider delegating tasks that drain your time and energy, whether household chores, administrative duties, or professional responsibilities. Identify trusted individuals or services to whom you can hand over these tasks, freeing up valuable time to focus on what truly matters to you.

What will you be outsourcing and sharing, and to whom?

Go deep into the specifics of your outsourcing and sharing strategy, considering the unique needs and preferences that shape your decision-making process. Whether hiring a virtual assistant to manage your inbox, enlisting the help of a meal delivery service, or partnering with a colleague on a collaborative project, tailor your approach to align with your goals and priorities. By strategically outsourcing and sharing tasks, you optimise your resources and create space for meaningful pursuits that ignite your passion and purpose.

What would you like to spend more time on?

Reflect on the activities and endeavours that bring you joy and fulfilment—those moments where you feel most alive and inspired. Consider what makes you sparkle, whether pursuing a creative passion, spending quality time with loved ones, or investing in personal growth and self-care. By identifying your sparkle moments, you gain clarity on where to allocate your time and energy, prioritising activities that nourish your soul and fuel your sense of purpose.

What 'sparkle enablers' could help you on your way?

Explore the resources, tools, and support systems that can propel you towards your sparkle moments. Think of them as sparkle enablers. From technology solutions that streamline your workflow to mentorship programmes that provide guidance and accountability, use everything that can amplify your efforts and accelerate your progress. Surround yourself with people and resources that uplift and inspire you, cultivating a nurturing environment that fosters growth and achievement.

In the following chapters, we'll delve deeper into each aspect of the ABCD framework, exploring practical strategies and actionable insights that empower you to live brighter and unlock your fullest potential. Together, we'll crack the code of smart living and embark on a transformative journey towards a life of purpose, passion, and possibility.

Chapter 3
Acceptance and Assessment

Mastering the Art

In the journey towards smart living, mastery begins with acceptance — a humble acknowledgement of our humanity and an unwavering embrace of our strengths and limitations. In this pivotal chapter, we embark on a transformative exploration of acceptance and assessment, empowering us to unlock our full potential and thrive in every aspect of our lives.

Acceptance: embracing your imperfections and your authenticity

At the outset of our smart living journey, we confront a fundamental truth: we are not superheroes. Despite the pressure to be Superwoman, we acknowledge that striving for perfection is unrealistic and unsustainable — a relentless pursuit that exacts a toll on our well-being and relationships. Instead, we embrace our imperfections, recognising that authenticity and vulnerability are the cornerstones of true strength.

Accept who you are, your strengths, and your limitations. In a world that celebrates achievement and success, succumbing to the pressure to excel in every aspect of our lives is easy. However, true empowerment lies in embracing our unique gifts and talents and celebrating the qualities that set us apart. By cultivating a deep self-awareness and self-compassion, we liberate ourselves from the shackles of comparison and self-doubt, paving the way for personal growth and fulfilment.

An honest review of your capabilities and priorities will help you identify what you need members of your 'personal team' to help with. Modern life presents many demands and responsibilities, each vying for our time and attention. In this context, strategic outsourcing becomes a powerful tool for maximising our time and energy and focusing on what truly matters. What are our essential tasks? What are just peripheral distractions?

Ask yourself: Why am I spending so much time doing this? Is it a priority for me? Or am I better off resting and recharging instead? In the pursuit of smart living, every decision carries weight, shaping the trajectory of our lives and defining our sense of fulfilment. By cultivating a discerning mindset and prioritising self-care, we empower ourselves to make choices that honour our well-being and align with our long-term goals.

The following pages delve deeper into the intricacies of acceptance and assessment, exploring practical strategies for embracing our authenticity and maximising our strengths. Together, we'll unlock the power of self-awareness and self-compassion, paving the way for a life defined by purpose, passion, and possibility.

Establishing your baseline

How do you currently spend your time?

It's a question that may catch you off guard, but understanding the answer is fundamental to living intentionally and prioritising the activities that bring you joy and fulfilment.

While your activities may vary weekly, maintaining a diary of your daily activities over a week can provide valuable insights into your 'time and motion.' By documenting how you allocate your time, you better understand where your energy is directed and whether your current activities align with your priorities and values.

For instance, let's consider gardening. On reflection, perhaps you will find that tasks such as mowing the lawns and trimming the hedges could be outsourced, allowing you to focus your time and energy on activities such as planting and tending to shrubs and flowers—tasks that embody your value of nurturing and give you joy.

In practical terms, this could mean hiring a gardening service to handle routine maintenance tasks, freeing up your time to immerse yourself in the aspects of gardening that bring you the most pleasure and satisfaction.

As we delve deeper into the journey of smart living, we'll explore practical strategies for making the best use of your time and aligning your activities with your priorities and values. Together, we'll unlock the secrets of intentional living and embark on a transformative journey towards a life defined by authenticity, purpose, and fulfilment.

Computing your hourly value

When freed from mundane and time-consuming tasks, your time is a precious commodity that can be dedicated to more valuable activities. But before you can make informed decisions about outsourcing tasks, you must first understand its value.

In this context, computing refers to calculating your time's hourly cost, providing a framework for evaluating the return on your time investment. By understanding the value of your time, you can determine whether outsourcing daily or weekly tasks is a financially sound decision.

To compute the hourly value of your time, divide your annual income by the total number of your work hours.

Sparkle

Let's break it down with an example:

If you earn £50,000 a year for a 40-hour week, you are paid for 40 hours, 52 weeks a year, which works out to 260 days or 2080 hours per year.

This works out as £50,000 ÷ 2080 = £24.03 per hour.

This means that, on average, an hour of your time is potentially worth £24.03. Of course, this calculation simplifies the reality of your hourly value. Other factors, such as commuting time and even company social events, may mean your work-related hours are more than this. For simplicity, we'll focus on core working hours for this example.

Now, consider any task costing less than £24.03 per hour. These tasks have a lower value than your time. Also, consider the time it takes you to complete the task compared to someone you could outsource it to. For instance, while it may take you six hours to deep clean your home, an experienced cleaner may accomplish the same task in just two hours at a fraction of the hourly cost for your time. Additionally, outsourcing to a professional cleaner ensures a higher quality result, further enhancing the value of your time investment.

Obviously, it would be best to cover your essential costs first and foremost. But if you have spare income or opportunities to earn overtime, this calculation may help you evaluate your options for outsourcing onerous tasks.

What makes you 'sparkle'?

Take a moment to analyse your current life — what brings a smile to your face, and what leaves you feeling disheartened? Reflect on the moments that delight you and light you up, igniting a sense of joy and fulfilment within you. Consider what activities you would pursue repeatedly if time and unintended consequences were not a concern.

Only you can determine what truly makes you happy. Whether spending quality time with loved ones, pursuing a passion project, or immersing yourself in a favourite hobby, your sources of happiness are as unique as you are. By exploring what brings you genuine joy and satisfaction, you gain insight into the activities that make life meaningful and fulfilling.

When considering what makes you happy and 'sparkle,' evaluating your work-life balance is essential. Are you devoting enough time and energy to activities outside of work that bring you joy and fulfilment? Regularly reviewing your priorities allows you to adjust and recalibrate in response to life events and changes, ensuring that your time and energy are aligned with your values and aspirations.

In practical terms, this may involve scheduling regular check-ins with yourself to assess your current state of happiness and fulfilment. Take time to engage in activities that nourish your soul and cultivate a sense of well-being, whether in nature, practising mindfulness, or connecting with friends and family.

Which tasks do you want to do?

When considering which tasks to delegate and which to retain for yourself, it's essential to start by analysing what brings you the most joy and fulfilment and what aligns with your available time. For example, while routine gardening was given as a potential choice for outsourcing in our earlier example, many of us find immense joy and tranquillity in tending our gardens. For those who do, gardening is a therapeutic activity that nourishes our souls and enhances our well-being.

Similarly, healthy cooking with personally selected ingredients may be considered non-negotiable by those of us who enjoy seeking inspiration from cookbooks and social media for new recipes and ideas, as well as preparing nutritious meals from scratch. This allows us to express our creativity in the kitchen and connect more deeply with the food we consume.

Ultimately, decisions about which tasks to handle yourself and which to outsource depend on your unique preferences, priorities, and circumstances. By aligning your choices with what brings you joy and fulfilment, you can ensure that your time and energy are invested in activities that enrich your life and contribute to your overall well-being.

What could you outsource?

To thine own self be true — know your strengths and weaknesses. With this guiding principle in mind, you can identify tasks that could be outsourced to free up your time and energy for activities that align more closely with your passions and priorities.

You could create a 'long list' of tasks you want to outsource. Many professional services now support different aspects of our busy lives. Examples of work-related tasks are:

Potential Item	Rationale
Administrative tasks	Outsourcing administrative tasks to a virtual assistant or administrative support service can help streamline your work and free up time for more important priorities.
Event planning	Planning events such as corporate gatherings can be time-consuming and stressful. Outsourcing event planning to a professional event planner can save you time and ensure that your event is executed flawlessly.
IT support	If you encounter technical issues with your computer, smartphone, or other devices, outsourcing IT support to a professional technician (if you don't already have support through work) can help you resolve problems quickly and efficiently, minimising downtime and frustration.
Transportation	Whether it's commuting to work, running errands, or travelling for leisure, outsourcing transportation tasks to a taxi or rideshare service can save you time and eliminate the hassle of driving and parking.

Sparkle

Examples of home-related tasks are:

Potential Item	Rationale
Gardening	It's more cost-effective and efficient to hire a professional gardener.
Grocery shopping	Online shopping for a home delivery can save you time and eliminate the need to navigate crowded stores and long checkout lines.
Home maintenance	DIY type tasks such as general maintenance can be outsourced to professional service providers.
Home organisation / Decluttering	A professional organiser can help you streamline your space and create systems for maintaining order.
House cleaning	The time and effort required for regular cleaning tasks can be significant. Outsourcing house cleaning to a professional cleaning service can free up time for other activities and help ensure that your home remains clean and organised.
Meal preparation	Outsourcing meal preparation to a meal delivery service can save time and effort while still ensuring that you have access to healthy and delicious meals (if you order healthy options!).
Personal grooming	Most professional women routinely outsource many aspects of personal grooming, such as nail and brow care, to professionals, saving us time and effort while ensuring that we look and feel our best.
Pet care	Services such as dog walking, pet sitting, and grooming can be outsourced to professional pet care providers, allowing you to ensure that your furry friends receive the care and attention they need even when you're busy.

By outsourcing these tasks, you can free up valuable time and energy to focus on activities that bring you joy, fulfilment, and success.

Empowering actions: applying acceptance and assessment

As we conclude our exploration of mastering the art of acceptance and assessment, we must recognise that embracing your strengths and limitations is the first step towards living a life of purpose and fulfilment. By accepting who you are and what you value, you empower yourself to make purposeful choices that align with your priorities and aspirations.

Here are five actions that you can take immediately to start applying the principles of acceptance and assessment:

1. **Conduct a self-assessment:** Reflect on your strengths, weaknesses, and values. Identify areas of your life where you excel and areas where you may need support or improvement. Use this self-awareness to inform your decisions and actions moving forward.

2. **Define your priorities:** Clarify what matters most to you, whether it's your career, relationships, health, or personal growth. Prioritise these areas based on their importance, and allocate your time and energy accordingly.

3. **Create a 'long list' of tasks:** Compile a list of tasks and responsibilities you currently handle yourself and those you could outsource. Consider the

value of your time and the benefits of delegating specific tasks to others.

4. **Take action:** Choose one task from your 'long list' that you can immediately delegate or outsource to free up your time and energy. Whether hiring a cleaner, delegating administrative tasks, or outsourcing home maintenance, taking action will help you experience the benefits of smart living firsthand.

5. **Practise self-compassion:** Remember that embracing acceptance means being kind to yourself and acknowledging that asking for help is okay. Practise self-compassion as you navigate the process of delegating tasks and making changes in your life. Celebrate your progress and recognise the courage it takes to embrace smart living.

By taking these actions, you'll be well on your way to mastering the art of acceptance and assessment, empowering yourself to live a life aligned with your values, priorities, and aspirations.

Chapter 4
Boundaries for Smart Living

Setting the stage

Boundaries are the essential limits and rules we establish in relationships and interactions. A person with healthy boundaries can confidently say 'no' when necessary and respect others' boundaries by accepting their 'no'. Healthy boundaries make it easier to maintain mutually supportive relationships and foster a sense of community.

I'm particularly drawn to Pastor Jerry Eze's teachings on this subject:

"Know when to stop, know when to start, know when to begin, know when to end, know when to talk, know when to shut up, know when to show up."

Boundaries serve as a framework through which we teach others to respect our energy and personal space. When we lack healthy boundaries, we risk overcommitting and

Sparkle

becoming overwhelmed, making it difficult to live smartly and prioritise the people and activities that bring us joy.

Setting boundaries empowers us to maintain control over our time and energy, allowing us to live more intentionally and authentically. Defining our boundaries creates a foundation for healthy relationships and establishes balance and harmony.

Practical applications:

1. Social boundaries: Communicate your needs and preferences to friends and family to ensure your social interactions align with your values and priorities. It's okay to decline invitations or limit your time with certain people if it helps preserve your energy and well-being.

2. Emotional boundaries: Recognise when you need space or time alone to recharge emotionally and communicate this need to others without feeling guilty. Practise assertive communication techniques to express your feelings and boundaries effectively, and don't hesitate to seek support from trusted friends or professionals when needed.

By defining and maintaining healthy boundaries in all areas of our lives, we cultivate a greater sense of self-awareness, self-respect, and empowerment.

Being clear about our values

Values are the guiding principles that reflect our beliefs, priorities, and what we consider important in life. They serve as an inner compass, directing our decisions, actions, and interactions with others. Understanding and aligning with our values enables us to live authentically and pursue a meaningful and fulfilling life.

Types of values:

1. Personal values: These are the beliefs and principles that are deeply important to us as individuals. Personal values may include integrity, honesty, compassion, resilience, and authenticity.

2. Social values encompass our beliefs about society, community, and the greater good. Social values include justice, equality, empathy, and environmental stewardship.

3. Professional values: In the context of work and career, professional values shape our behaviour, ethics, and standards of conduct. These values may include professionalism, accountability, teamwork, and continuous learning.

4. Cultural Values: Our cultural background, traditions, and upbringing influence cultural values. They shape our worldviews, attitudes, and behaviours within a cultural context.

Practical applications:

1. Integrity: When we value integrity, we uphold honesty and integrity in all our interactions, personally and professionally, even when faced with difficult decisions or challenges.

2. Compassion: When we value compassion, we demonstrate empathy and kindness toward others and take action to alleviate the suffering of those in need.

3. Work-life balance: When we value our work-life balance, we prioritise time with family, self-care, and leisure activities to maintain a healthy balance between work and personal life.

4. Environmental stewardship: When we value environmental stewardship, we adopt eco-friendly practices, reducing waste and conserving natural resources to protect the environment for future generations.

5. Growth mindset: When we value a growth mindset, we embrace opportunities for learning and personal growth, approaching challenges with optimism and resilience.

Being clear about our values allows us to make decisions aligned with our beliefs and aspirations, leading to a more fulfilling and purposeful life. By living by our values, we cultivate a sense of authenticity, integrity, and inner peace.

Taking action towards smart living

As we conclude this chapter, it's time to take actionable steps towards implementing these principles in our lives. Establishing clear boundaries and identifying our core values pave the way for living authentically and intentionally. Here are five actions that you can take immediately to start incorporating these concepts into your daily life:

1. Reflect on your boundaries: Reflect on your personal and professional boundaries. Consider areas where you may need to set firmer limits or communicate your boundaries more clearly to others. Write down specific boundaries you want to establish and commit to enforcing them.

2. Identify your core values: Reflect on what truly matters to you in life and identify your core values. Consider the principles and beliefs that guide your decisions and actions. Please write down your top values and use them as a compass to navigate your choices and priorities.

3. Communicate your boundaries and values: Take proactive steps to communicate your boundaries and values to those around you. Clearly articulate your needs, preferences, and non-negotiables in

Sparkle

relationships, work, and other areas of your life. Practise assertive communication techniques to express yourself effectively and respectfully.

4. Set boundaries in daily life: Implement practical boundaries in your daily routines and interactions. Schedule regular self-care activities, prioritise tasks based on their importance and urgency, and learn to say 'no' to requests or commitments that do not align with your values or priorities.

5. Align your actions with your values: Make a conscious effort to align your actions with your core values. Reflect on how your daily choices and behaviours reflect your values and make adjustments as needed. Strive to live authentically and in alignment with what truly matters to you.

By taking these actions, you'll be well on your way to cultivating a life guided by clear boundaries and meaningful values.

Chapter 5
Thriving Together

Leveraging the strength of your community

In the pursuit of smarter living, the strength of the community plays a pivotal role in supporting and enriching our lives. A community is a collective of individuals who share common interests, values, or characteristics, and it serves as a source of mutual support, connection, and collaboration. For a professional woman, her community may encompass various types of relationships and networks, each offering unique benefits and opportunities for growth.

Types of community:

1. Personal community: This includes friends, family members, and close acquaintances who provide emotional support, companionship, and shared experiences. Personal communities offer a sense of belonging and connection, nurturing

Sparkle

relationships that contribute to our well-being and happiness.

2. Professional community: As professionals, we may also belong to networks and associations within our industries or fields of expertise. These communities provide opportunities for networking, skill development, and career advancement. Professional communities offer a platform for collaboration, knowledge sharing, and mentorship, enabling us to thrive in our careers.

3. Local community: engaging with our neighbours, regional organisations, and community groups fosters a sense of belonging and civic engagement. Local communities offer opportunities for social interaction, shared resources, and collective action to address common issues and concerns. From Neighbourhood Watch groups to community gardens, these connections contribute to the vitality and resilience of our neighbourhoods.

Practical applications:

1. Mutual support: establishing a mutual support system within your community can provide invaluable assistance during challenging times. For example, arranging a babysitting co-op with

friends allows parents to share childcare responsibilities, giving each other much-needed breaks and support.

2. Networking events: Actively participating in professional networking events, conferences, and industry gatherings enables us to expand our professional community and cultivate valuable connections. This may result in opportunities to collaborate with others, find a mentor, and progress in our careers.

3. Community initiatives: Getting involved in local community initiatives, such as volunteering for a neighbourhood clean-up or joining a community garden project, strengthens our bonds with our neighbours and fosters a sense of collective responsibility and pride in our community.

4. Online communities: Engaging in online forums, social media groups, and virtual communities related to specific interests or hobbies allows us to connect with like-minded people worldwide. Online communities offer opportunities for knowledge sharing, peer support, and collaboration.

By leveraging the strength of community in all its forms, as a professional woman, you can tap into a diverse

Sparkle

network of support, resources, and opportunities for personal and professional growth.

Network audit

Conducting a network audit involves assessing the relationships and connections in your personal and professional networks to evaluate their value and contribution to your life. This process helps you identify strengths, weaknesses, opportunities, and potential areas for improvement in your network. By understanding the dynamics of your network, you can make informed decisions about cultivating and leveraging your connections more effectively.

An example of a network audit could be:

Relationship	Strengths	Weaknesses	Opportunities
Professional contacts	Industry insights, career support	Limited personal connection	Networking for career growth
Online communities	Knowledge sharing, diverse perspectives	Limited face-to-face interaction	Opportunities for learning and collaboration

Practical applications:

1. Assess your relationships: Take an inventory of the relationships in your personal and professional networks. Consider each connection's strengths and weaknesses and the value it brings to your life

regarding emotional support, expertise, resources, and opportunities.

2. Identify areas for improvement: Reflect on areas where your network may be lacking or where you could benefit from expanding your connections. Look for opportunities to diversify your network by contacting people with different backgrounds, perspectives, and skill sets.

3. Nurture meaningful connections: Prioritise relationships that add value to your life and invest time and effort in nurturing them. Cultivate authentic connections based on mutual respect, trust, and shared interests online and offline.

4. Seek feedback: Consider seeking input from trusted friends, mentors, or colleagues about your network and how to strengthen it. They may offer valuable insights and suggestions for expanding your network and maximising its potential.

By conducting a network audit, you will better understand the strengths and weaknesses of your relationships and how they contribute to your personal and professional growth. This will enable you to make strategic decisions about leveraging and cultivating your network to achieve your goals and thrive in all aspects of your life.

Sparkle

Taking action towards community thriving

As we conclude this chapter, it's time to take actionable steps towards building and nurturing meaningful connections in our lives. By harnessing the power of community, we can create a support system that empowers us to thrive together. Here are five actions that you can take immediately to cultivate and make the most of the communities you belong to:

1. Conduct a network audit: Take an inventory of your personal and professional networks to assess their strengths, weaknesses, and opportunities for growth. Identify areas where you can diversify and expand your connections to enhance your support system.

2. Reach out to your connections: Take proactive steps to reconnect with people in your network you haven't seen in a while. Schedule coffee meetings, phone calls, or virtual catch-ups to strengthen relationships and explore potential collaboration opportunities.

3. Join community initiatives: Get involved in local community initiatives, events, or groups that align with your interests and values. Volunteer for community projects, attend neighbourhood meetings or join online forums to connect with like-minded people and contribute to your community's well-being.

4. Offer support to others: Extend a helping hand to members of your community who may require support or assistance. Whether offering a listening ear, providing practical help, or sharing resources, small acts of kindness can strengthen bonds and foster a sense of belonging within your community.

5. Express gratitude: Take time to express gratitude to the members of your community who have supported and uplifted you. Send a heartfelt thank-you note, express appreciation in person, or reach out to let them know how much their presence means to you.

By taking these actions, you'll be actively contributing to the strength and vitality of your community while building deeper connections with those around you.

Chapter 6
Decision Making

Mastering the art of Making the Call

Mastering the art of decision-making is paramount in the journey of smarter living. Deciding involves weighing your options, prioritising your commitments, and aligning your actions with your values and goals. It's an opportunity to carefully balance competing priorities, ensuring that your choices contribute to your overall well-being and fulfilment.

Types of decisions:

1. Strategic outsourcing: Decide which tasks or responsibilities you will outsource to others to free up your time and energy for more meaningful pursuits. Whether you hire a virtual assistant for administrative tasks or delegate household chores to a cleaning service, strategic outsourcing allows

you to focus on activities that align with your strengths and priorities.

2. Time allocation: Determine how you will allocate your time and attention to various aspects of your life, including work, family, hobbies, and self-care. Identify the activities and people that bring you joy and fulfilment, and prioritise them in your schedule to ensure a balanced and fulfilling life.

3. Investment in relationships: Invest in relationships that align with your values and contribute positively to your life. Decide which connections are worth nurturing and prioritise quality time with loved ones, friends, and mentors who support and inspire you.

Practical applications:

1. **Clarify your priorities:** Reflect on your values, goals, and priorities. Clearly define what matters most to you in both your personal and professional life. Understanding your priorities will guide you in making decisions that align with your aspirations.

2. **Evaluate your options:** When faced with a decision, thoroughly assess the available options and their potential outcomes. Consider each choice's short-term and long-term implications, weighing the risks and benefits before deciding.

Sparkle

3. **Seek input:** When making important decisions, don't hesitate to seek feedback from trusted mentors, friends, or colleagues. Gathering diverse perspectives can provide valuable insights and help you make more informed choices.

4. **Trust your intuition:** When making decisions, pay attention to your intuition and gut instincts. While gathering information and analysing data is essential, sometimes your instincts can offer valuable guidance that logic alone cannot provide.

5. **Take action:** Once you've decided, take decisive action to implement it. Avoid second-guessing yourself or dwelling on uncertainty. Trust in your ability to make sound decisions and commit to moving forward confidently.

Chapter 7
Sparkle Enablers

I have included this chapter because living a smarter and more fulfilling life does not happen by chance. Identifying and utilising the power of sparkle enablers is crucial - those gems that act as catalysts for your personal growth and overall well-being. Sparkle enablers are the tools, practices, and resources that support achieving your goals and living a more fulfilling life.

Types of sparkle enablers:

1. Leadership: Cultivating leadership skills is essential for navigating life's challenges and inspiring others to do the same. Effective leadership is a cornerstone of smart living, whether we lead ourselves with self-discipline and resilience or lead others with empathy and vision.

2. Smart technology: Embracing smart tools and technology can streamline our daily tasks, optimise our productivity, and enhance our overall efficiency. From time management apps to

Sparkle

smart home devices, leveraging technology can create a smarter environment that supports your goals and aspirations.

3. Mindfulness and nature's jewels: Mindfulness and connecting with nature are powerful ways to cultivate inner peace, clarity, and resilience. Spending time outdoors, practising meditation, or engaging in mindful activities can help us reduce stress, enhance our mental well-being, and foster a deeper connection with ourselves and the world around us.

4. Emotional intelligence: Developing emotional intelligence is key to building strong relationships, managing stress, and making sound decisions. We can enhance our personal and professional success by honing our ability to understand and regulate our emotions, empathising with others, and navigating interpersonal dynamics effectively.

5. Glow-up plan: Self-care, encompassing physical, mental, emotional, and spiritual well-being, is an essential component of smart living. We can promote our holistic health and resilience by creating a 'glow-up' plan that prioritises self-care practices such as exercise, healthy eating, mindfulness, and self-reflection.

Practical actions:

1. Leadership workshops: Attend workshops or seminars to enhance your leadership skills and gain valuable insights into effective leadership practices.

2. Smart home devices: Invest in smart home devices such as smart thermostats, lighting systems, or virtual assistants to automate tasks and create a more efficient living environment.

3. Nature walks: Take regular nature walks or hikes to immerse yourself in the beauty of the natural world and reap the therapeutic benefits of spending time outdoors.

4. Emotional intelligence training: Participate in training programmes or workshops to develop essential emotional intelligence skills such as self-awareness, self-regulation, and empathy.

5. Self-care rituals: Establish daily self-care rituals such as morning meditation, journaling, or exercise routines to nurture your physical, mental, and emotional well-being.

Leadership

Leadership as a sparkle enabler

Leadership is a potent enabler, illuminating the path toward personal growth, resilience, and success. Whether we lead ourselves with self-discipline and purpose or inspire others with vision and empathy, leadership skills are essential for navigating life's complexities and thriving in both personal and professional spheres.

Types of leadership:

1. Self-leadership: To lead ourselves and achieve our goals and aspirations, we must build self-awareness, self-discipline, and self-motivation. We must set clear objectives, manage our time effectively, and maintain our resilience in facing challenges. Practising self-leadership empowers us to take ownership of our lives and chart a course toward success.

Example: Set aside time each morning for goal-setting and reflection so you can prioritise your tasks and align your daily actions with your long-term aspirations. This will maximise your productivity and fulfilment.

2. Leading others: In leading others, we must inspire, empower, and support them to achieve the goals and objectives we all share. This depends on fostering trust, collaboration, and accountability within work teams or communities. Effective leadership cultivates a culture of inclusivity, innovation, and excellence, enabling individuals to thrive and contribute their best.

Example: As a manager, you can build a supportive work environment by actively listening to employees' concerns, recognising their contributions, and providing opportunities for growth and development. By fostering a culture of trust and empowerment, you will inspire your team to excel and achieve shared goals.

Practical actions:

1. Leadership development programmes: Participate in leadership development programmes or workshops to enhance your leadership skills and gain valuable insights into effective leadership practices. These programmes often provide opportunities for self-assessment, skill-building exercises, and peer learning, empowering participants to become more impactful leaders.

2. Mentorship relationships: Seek mentorship from experienced leaders or peers who can provide guidance, feedback, and support in your leadership journey. Have regular mentorship conversations with them, seek their advice on your challenges or opportunities, and use their expertise to accelerate your growth as a leader.

3. Volunteer leadership roles: Volunteer for leadership roles in community organisations, professional associations, or charitable initiatives. Leading volunteer projects or committees allows

you to hone your leadership skills, expand your network, and positively impact causes you care about.

As a sparkle enabler, leadership can unlock your leadership potential, inspire others, and create positive change in your life and communities. Through self-leadership and leading others, you can confidently navigate challenges, foster collaboration, and cultivate a culture of excellence and empowerment.

Smart technology

Smart technology as a sparkle enabler

In today's digital age, smart technology serves as a potent sparkle enabler, revolutionising how we interact with our environment and enhancing efficiency, convenience, and comfort. From smart thermostats to connected appliances, these innovative tools empower us to live smarter, more streamlined lives and create environments that support our well-being and productivity.

Practical applications:

1. Smart thermostats: Smart thermostats like Nest or Ecobee enable us to regulate our homes' temperature and optimise energy usage remotely. They promote energy efficiency and comfort, supporting our well-being and productivity while reducing utility costs.

2. Smart doorbells: With features like video streaming and motion detection, smart doorbells like Ring or Nest Hello provide enhanced security and convenience, whether we are at home or elsewhere.

3. Smart lights: Smart lighting systems, such as Philips Hue or LIFX, allow us to customise the lighting in our homes, enhancing our comfort and productivity.

4. Smart locks: Smart locks like August or Schlage Encode offer keyless entry and remote access capabilities. They allow users to lock and unlock their doors from anywhere via a mobile app. With features like temporary virtual keys and activity logs, smart locks provide enhanced security and convenience, allowing us to grant guests or service providers remote access.

5. Smart refrigerators: Smart refrigerators, such as Samsung Family Hub or LG InstaView, feature built-in touchscreens, cameras, and Wi-Fi connectivity. They allow us to manage groceries, view recipes, and stream entertainment content. With features like food inventory tracking and expiration alerts, smart refrigerators help us organise our shopping, minimise food waste, and streamline meal planning.

6. Smart time management applications: Apps like "Motion" harness automation and artificial intelligence can schedule activities and build to-do lists.

Mindfulness

Mindfulness and nature's jewels

Mindfulness:

Mindfulness involves being fully present and engaged in the present moment without judgment or distraction. It entails slowing down and cultivating awareness of our thoughts, emotions, and sensations. By embracing mindfulness, we can develop greater clarity, focus, and emotional resilience, essential for making informed decisions, including those that will increase our sparkle.

Nature's jewels:

Nature's jewels are the exquisite wonders of the natural world that inspire awe and appreciation. These simple yet profound experiences connect us with the beauty and vitality of the natural environment. From the delicate dewdrops on a spider's web to the majestic dance of trees in the wind, nature's jewels encompass a wide array of sensory delights freely available daily.

Practical examples:

1. Dew on a spider's web: Witnessing the glistening dewdrops on a spider's web after a morning mist can evoke a sense of wonder and tranquillity, reminding us of the intricate beauty of nature's creations.

2. Birdsong: Listening to the melodious chirping of birds in the early morning or at dusk can uplift our spirits and foster a deep connection with the natural world.

3. Red sky at night: Observing the vivid hues of a sunset or sunrise, such as a red sky at night, can evoke a sense of awe and appreciation for the sky's ever-changing canvas.

4. Full moon: Gazing up at the luminous glow of a full moon illuminating the night sky can inspire contemplation and evoke a sense of wonder at the vastness of the universe.

5. The smell of a rose: Inhaling the delicate fragrance of a blooming rose or the earthy scent of freshly cut grass can evoke a sense of grounding and rejuvenation, reconnecting us with the sensory pleasures of nature.

Professional women can foster inner peace, resilience and creativity by practising mindfulness and immersing themselves in nature's beauty. These practices enhance well-being and provide valuable perspective and inspiration for navigating life's challenges and decisions, including those related to living smarter and increasing our sparkle.

Emotional intelligence

Emotional intelligence as a sparkle enabler

Emotional intelligence is crucial for navigating the complexities of human interaction and decision-making. It encompasses the ability to recognise, understand, and manage both our own emotions and those of others, leading to more effective communication, empathy, and conflict resolution.

Practical applications:

1. Recognising emotions: Identifying and acknowledging our feelings in various situations allows us to respond thoughtfully rather than impulsively. For example, recognising when we are becoming overwhelmed or stressed can prompt us to take proactive steps to manage our workload or seek support from others.

2. Empathy: Empathy involves putting ourselves in others' shoes and understanding their perspectives and feelings. When outsourcing tasks, having empathy enables us to consider how our decisions

may impact others and to communicate our needs and expectations effectively. For instance, empathising with a colleague's workload may lead us to offer assistance or adjust deadlines accordingly.

3. Conflict resolution: Emotional intelligence equips us with the skills to navigate conflicts constructively and find mutually beneficial solutions. Outsourcing may involve addressing disagreements or misunderstandings with service providers or collaborators in a respectful and empathetic manner and fostering trust and cooperation.

Emotional deposits:

As Stephen Covey describes them, emotional deposits refer to the actions and behaviours that build trust and goodwill in relationships, akin to deposits made into an emotional bank account. By consistently demonstrating courtesy, honesty, and reliability, we accumulate trust and rapport with others, enhancing our ability to collaborate and delegate tasks effectively.

Emotional Deposits

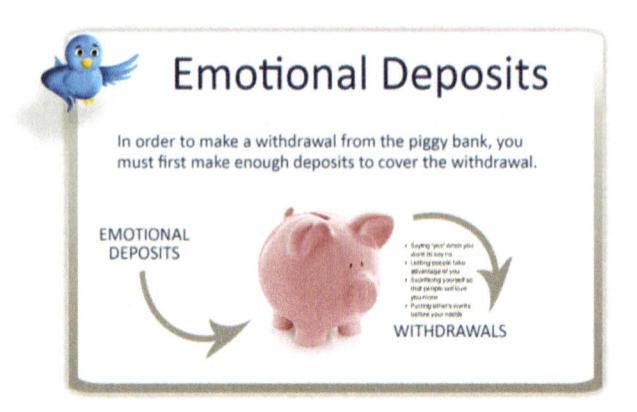

In order to make a withdrawal from the piggy bank, you must first make enough deposits to cover the withdrawal.

Practical applications:

1. Keeping commitments: When we follow through on our promises and obligations, we demonstrate reliability and integrity, contributing to a positive emotional balance in our relationships. For instance, meeting deadlines and fulfilling obligations in professional partnerships strengthens trust and fosters a conducive environment for outsourcing.

2. Showing respect: Respecting others' perspectives, boundaries, and contributions fosters mutual respect and goodwill. By acknowledging and valuing the expertise and efforts of service providers or collaborators, we contribute to a supportive and collaborative atmosphere conducive to successful outsourcing.

3. Expressing appreciation: Expressing gratitude and appreciation for the contributions of others nurtures a culture of positivity and encouragement. Recognising service providers' or team members' efforts and achievements strengthens bonds and encourages continued collaboration and support.

By developing emotional intelligence and consistently investing in our relationships, professional women can lay the foundation for effective outsourcing and shared endeavours by fostering trust, empathy, and collaboration.

Self-care and glow-up plans

Self-care and glow-up plans as sparkle enablers

Self-care encompasses a comprehensive approach to nurturing and maintaining our overall well-being, addressing our lives' physical, mental, emotional, spiritual, and personalised aspects. It is essential for promoting our health, resilience, and positive mindset, which are key to effective decision-making and pursuing personal and professional goals. Without a commitment to self-care, we may experience heightened stress, burnout, and a diminished capacity to thrive.

Practical applications:

1. Physical self-care: Regular exercise, eating nutritious foods, staying hydrated, and getting adequate rest are fundamental aspects of physical self-care. These practices improve energy levels, physical health, and overall vitality, enabling us to approach our daily tasks with greater vigour and efficiency.

2. Mental and emotional self-care: Practices such as mindfulness meditation, journalling, seeking therapy or counselling, and engaging in hobbies or activities that bring joy and relaxation are essential for nurturing our mental and emotional well-being. Taking time to process our emotions, manage our stress, and cultivate our resilience enhances our emotional intelligence and fosters a balanced mindset conducive to effective decision-making.

3. Spiritual self-care: For some of us, spiritual practices such as prayer, meditation, or spending time in nature are integral to our self-care routines. These practices provide opportunities for reflection, connection with inner values, and a sense of purpose, fostering a deeper understanding of fulfilment and inner peace.

4. Personalised self-care involves identifying and prioritising activities or practices uniquely tailored

to our needs and preferences. This may include activities related to our appearance, beauty rituals, creative pursuits, or any other endeavours contributing to our personal growth, confidence, and self-expression.

Glow-up plan:

A glow-up plan is a structured framework for consistently focusing on self-care and personal development. It involves setting specific goals and incorporating regular self-care practices into daily routines. By checking in with ourselves regularly and adjusting the glow-up plan, we can ensure we prioritise our well-being and nurture our inner sparkle.

Chapter 8
GLOW UP!

In executive coaching, the GROW coaching model stands out for its goal-oriented approach and emphasis on intentionality. GROW stands for Goals, Reality, Options (what could you do?), and Will (what will you do?), providing a structured framework for personal growth and development. Inspired by this model, I have devised the glow-up plan to help us all add sparkle to our lives.

Glow-up essentials

These are the seven essentials for your holistic glow-up plan to help you achieve everyday sparkle.

1. Nutritional wellness
2. Sleep hygiene
3. Time management
4. Financial wellness
5. Relationship nourishment
6. Creativity and expression

7. Environmental wellness

Nutritional wellness

Maintaining a balanced diet is the cornerstone of optimal health and well-being. What we consume directly affects our energy levels, mood, cognitive function, and physical vitality. Here's a closer look at why nutritional wellness matters and how you can make positive changes in your diet:

1. **Importance of a balanced diet:** A balanced diet provides essential nutrients, vitamins, minerals, and macronutrients that support overall health. It includes a variety of foods from different food groups, such as fruits, vegetables, whole grains, lean proteins, and healthy fats. By nourishing your body with diverse nutrients, you can support proper growth and development, maintain a healthy weight, and reduce the risk of chronic diseases like heart disease, diabetes, and obesity.

2. **Practical tips for healthier food choices:** Incorporating more nutritious food choices into your daily meals doesn't have to be complicated. Start by focusing on whole, unprocessed foods and minimising the intake of sugary drinks, processed snacks, and fast food. Here are some practical tips to consider:

- Fill half your plate with fruits and vegetables at each meal.
- Choose whole grains like brown rice, quinoa, and oats over refined grains.
- Opt for lean protein sources such as fish, poultry, beans, and tofu.
- Include healthy fats from nuts, seeds, avocados, and olive oil.
- Limit added sugars and salt in your diet, and read food labels to make informed choices.
- Stay hydrated by drinking plenty of water throughout the day.

3. **Benefits of meal planning and mindful eating:** Meal planning involves preparing and organising meals ahead of time, which can help you make healthier choices and save time during busy days. It allows you to create balanced meals, control portions, and avoid impulsive food choices. Practising mindful eating involves paying attention to your body's hunger and fullness cues, savouring each bite, and eating without distractions. This approach can help you develop a healthier relationship with food, prevent overeating, and enhance your enjoyment of meals.

Sleep hygiene

Quality sleep is essential for overall health and well-being, playing a vital role in physical, mental, and emotional functions. Here's why prioritising sleep hygiene is crucial, along with strategies to enhance the quality of your sleep:

1. **Significance of quality sleep:** Quality sleep is essential for numerous bodily functions, including cellular repair, immune function, hormone regulation, and cognitive processes such as memory consolidation and learning. Adequate sleep is also linked to better mood regulation, stress management, and overall mental health. Conversely, chronic sleep deprivation or poor sleep quality can increase the risk of health issues such as obesity, heart disease, diabetes, and mental health disorders like depression and anxiety.

2. **Strategies for improving sleep hygiene:** Improving sleep hygiene involves adopting habits and practices that promote restful and uninterrupted sleep. Here are some strategies to consider:

    - Establish a consistent sleep schedule by going to bed and waking up at the same time each day, even on weekends.
    - Create a relaxing bedtime routine to signal to your body that it's time to wind down. This could include reading, taking a warm bath, or

Sparkle

practising relaxation techniques such as deep breathing or meditation.

- Keep your bedroom cool, dark, and quiet to designate a comfortable and conducive sleep environment. Invest in a comfy mattress, pillows, and bedding to enhance comfort.
- Limit exposure to screens, such as smartphones, tablets, and computers, at least an hour before bedtime, as the blue light emitted can interfere with melatonin production and disrupt sleep.
- Avoid consuming caffeine, nicotine, and large meals close to bedtime, as these can interfere with sleep quality and disrupt your ability to fall asleep.
- Create a relaxing bedtime routine to signal to your body that it's time to wind down.

3. **Effects of technology and stress on sleep patterns:** The use of technology, such as smartphones, computers, and televisions, before bedtime can disrupt sleep patterns and interfere with the body's natural circadian rhythm. Additionally, stress and anxiety can lead to difficulty falling asleep or staying asleep, resulting in restless nights and daytime fatigue. To mitigate these effects, consider implementing strategies such as:

- We are establishing technology-free zones or implementing screen time limits in the hours leading up to bedtime.
- I am practising relaxation techniques, such as deep breathing, progressive muscle relaxation, or mindfulness meditation, to reduce stress and promote relaxation before sleep.
- Create a worry journal to write down any concerns or thoughts before bedtime. This will allow you to clear your mind and reduce bedtime anxiety.

Time management

Effective time management is a cornerstone of success, both personally and professionally. Here's a breakdown of its role, along with techniques and considerations for mastering this skill:

1. **Role of effective time management:** Effective time management is essential for achieving personal and professional goals. By efficiently allocating our time and resources, we can increase productivity, reduce stress, and accomplish more in less time. It involves identifying priorities, setting realistic goals, and implementing strategies to maximise efficiency and minimise distractions. With effective time management, we can better balance our

Sparkle

responsibilities, meet deadlines, and make progress toward our desired outcomes.

2. **Techniques for prioritising tasks:** Prioritising tasks is crucial for focusing on what matters most and avoiding the trap of busyness without productivity. Some techniques for prioritisation include:

    - Using the Eisenhower Matrix: Categorise tasks based on urgency and importance to determine which ones require immediate attention, delegation, scheduling, or elimination.

    - Applying the 80/20 Rule (Pareto Principle): Identify the 20% of tasks that yield 80% of the results and prioritise them accordingly.

    - Creating to-do lists: Compile a list of tasks and rank them based on their significance and deadlines, tackling high-priority items first.

3. **Setting boundaries**: Boundaries are vital for maintaining a healthy work-life balance and preventing burnout. Techniques for setting boundaries include:

    - Establishing clear work hours: If needed, specify your work hours and communicate them to colleagues and clients to prevent work from encroaching on your time.

- Saying no: Learn to decline requests or commitments that do not align with your priorities or goals, allowing you to focus on what matters most.
- Designating leisure time: Schedule regular breaks and leisure activities so you can recharge, relax, and pursue hobbies and interests outside of work.

4. **Optimising productivity:** Optimising productivity involves making the best use of tools, techniques, and habits to work smarter, not harder. Strategies for enhancing productivity include:
   - Time blocking: Allocate dedicated time blocks for specific tasks or activities to minimise distractions and maintain focus.
   - Implementing the Pomodoro Technique: Break work into intervals, typically 25 minutes of focused work followed by a short break, to enhance your concentration and productivity.
   - Eliminating multitasking: Focus on one task at a time to improve your efficiency and reduce cognitive overload, leading to better outcomes and higher-quality work.

5. **Importance of balance and leisure time:** Balance and leisure time are essential for preventing burnout, fostering creativity, and maintaining

overall well-being. By incorporating leisure activities and downtime into your schedule, you can recharge your batteries, reduce stress, and boost creativity. Whether spending time with loved ones, pursuing hobbies, or engaging in self-care practices, prioritising leisure time allows you to replenish your energy reserves and approach your responsibilities with renewed vigour and enthusiasm. Remember, achieving balance is not just about managing your time; it's also about managing your energy and prioritising your overall health and happiness.

Financial wellness

Financial wellness is critical to overall well-being, impacting our lives. Here's an exploration of its significance, along with practical advice for achieving financial health:

1. **Relationship between financial health and overall well-being:** Financial health influences many facets of our lives, including physical health, mental well-being, relationships, and overall quality of life. It affects our ability to meet basic needs, pursue opportunities, and cope with unexpected challenges. Financial stability provides a sense of security, reduces stress, and enables us to focus on personal growth and fulfilment.

2. **Guidance on budgeting, saving, and investing:** Budgeting and investing are fundamental to financial wellness. Here's how you can approach each of them:

    - **Budgeting:** Create a comprehensive budget that outlines your income, expenses, and savings goals. Track your spending habits, identify areas for potential savings, and prioritise essential expenses while cutting back on unnecessary ones.

    - **Saving:** Establish an emergency fund to cover unforeseen expenses and financial setbacks. Aim to save a percentage of your income regularly, automating savings contributions whenever possible. Consider setting specific savings goals for short-term purchases, such as vacations, and long-term objectives, such as home ownership or retirement.

    - **Investing:** Educate yourself about different investment options, such as stocks, bonds, mutual funds, and retirement accounts. Diversify your investment portfolio to manage risk effectively, and consider seeking professional advice to develop a personalised investment strategy aligned with your financial goals and risk tolerance.

Sparkle

3. **Psychological aspects of money management:** Money management involves practical considerations and psychological factors. Common psychological challenges that influence financial behaviour and decision-making include:

    - **Financial stress:** Address the emotional impact of economic stress and anxiety by acknowledging your feelings of fear, uncertainty, and shame. Practise mindfulness techniques, seek social support, and develop coping strategies to manage stress effectively.

    - **Money mindset:** Examine your beliefs, attitudes, and money-related behaviours. Challenge your limiting beliefs about wealth, success, and abundance, and cultivate a positive money mindset focused on abundance, gratitude, and financial empowerment.

    - **Delayed gratification:** Develop the self-discipline to prioritise your long-term financial goals over short-term pleasures. Practise self-control, set SMART (Specific, Measurable, Achievable, Relevant, Time-bound) goals, and reward yourself for progress toward financial milestones.

4. **Strategies for overcoming financial stress:** Overcoming financial stress requires proactive

steps to improve financial literacy, build resilience, and develop healthy coping mechanisms. Strategies for managing financial stress include:

- **Seeking financial education:** Enhance financial literacy by attending workshops, reading books, and accessing reputable online resources. Learn about budgeting, saving, investing, debt management, and financial planning.

- **Creating a support network:** Surround yourself with supportive individuals who can offer guidance, encouragement, and practical assistance during challenging times. Share your financial concerns with trusted friends, family members, or professionals who can provide perspective and advice.

- **Taking control of your finances:** Take proactive steps to address financial challenges, such as creating a debt repayment plan, negotiating with creditors, or exploring opportunities to increase income or reduce expenses. Focus on solutions rather than dwelling on problems, and celebrate small victories.

5. **Treat financial wellness as a journey:** Finally, recognise that achieving financial wellness is a

journey rather than a destination. Be patient with yourself, celebrate progress, and remain committed to continuous learning and improvement. Embrace a growth mindset that encourages resilience, adaptability, and resourcefulness in navigating life's financial challenges and opportunities. Remember, financial wellness is not just about accumulating wealth; it's about achieving a sense of security, freedom, and peace of mind that allows you to live a fulfilling and purposeful life.

Relationship nourishment

Nurturing meaningful connections with others is essential for personal growth, emotional well-being, and overall happiness. Here's an exploration of its significance and practical advice for fostering healthy relationships.

1. **Importance of nurturing meaningful connections:** Meaningful connections enrich our lives, providing emotional support, companionship, and a sense of belonging. Strong relationships contribute to our mental and physical health, reducing stress, anxiety, and depression while increasing our happiness and sense of fulfilment. Investing in relationships cultivates empathy, compassion, and understanding, fostering deeper connections with

others and enhancing the quality of our interactions.

2. **Tips for effective communication, conflict resolution, and boundary-setting:** Effective communication lays the foundation for healthy relationships, allowing us to express our thoughts, feelings, and needs openly and honestly. Here are some tips for improving communication, resolving conflicts constructively and setting boundaries:

- **Active listening:** Practise active listening by focusing on what the other person is saying without interrupting them or forming any judgment. Validate their feelings and perspectives to foster empathy and understanding.

- **Assertive communication:** Express yourself assertively, using 'I' statements to communicate your thoughts, feelings, and boundaries clearly and respectfully. Avoid passive or aggressive communication styles, leading to misunderstandings and resentment.

- **Conflict resolution:** Approach conflicts as opportunities for growth and understanding rather than as battles to be won. Listen actively, seek common ground, and collaborate with the other person to find mutually acceptable solutions. Be willing to compromise and apologise when necessary to preserve the relationship.

- **Boundary-setting:** Establish clear boundaries to protect your physical, emotional, and psychological well-being. Communicate your boundaries assertively and enforce them consistently, respecting others' boundaries while advocating for your needs and preferences.

3. **Benefits of building a support network:** a support network of trusted friends, family members, and colleagues can provide invaluable emotional support, practical assistance, and encouragement during challenging times. A strong support network can offer:

    - **Emotional support:** You can share your thoughts, feelings, and experiences with supportive individuals who offer empathy, validation, and perspective. Knowing you're not alone, you can lean on your support network during stress, grief, or uncertainty.
    - **Practical assistance:** When facing practical challenges or obstacles, you can seek help from your support network. Whether it's help with childcare, household chores, or

professional advice, your network can provide assistance and resources.

- **Encouragement and motivation:** By surrounding yourself with positive, uplifting people who believe in your potential, you can draw inspiration from their achievements, celebrate your successes together, and offer each other support during setbacks. They will encourage you to pursue your goals and aspirations.

4. **Investing in personal and professional relationships:** Investing in personal and professional relationships is essential for holistic well-being and success. Here's how to nurture relationships in both these spheres:

    - **Personal relationships:** Dedicate time and effort to maintaining and strengthening your relationships with your family, friends, and significant others. Plan regular quality time together, engage in meaningful conversations, and show appreciation for their presence in your life.

    - **Professional relationships:** Foster trust, mutual respect, and cooperation with colleagues, mentors, and collaborators to cultivate positive relationships. Offer support, recognition, and feedback to colleagues, build professional networks, and seek mentorship and career development opportunities.

Creativity and expression

Creativity is a powerful force that fuels our self-expression, fosters our personal growth, and enhances our overall well-being. Here's a closer look at its significance and the therapeutic benefits of creative expression.

1. **Role of creativity in enabling self-expression and personal fulfilment:** Creativity empowers us to express ourselves, tapping into our unique perspectives, emotions, and experiences. Whether through art, writing, music, or other means, creativity allows us to communicate our thoughts, feelings, and innermost desires in meaningful and impactful ways, giving us a sense of accomplishment and personal fulfilment.

2. **Exploring artistic outlets and hobbies:** Exploring artistic outlets and hobbies opens doors to new experiences, passions, and sources of joy. Whether painting, drawing, photography, crafting, cooking, gardening, or playing a musical instrument, engaging in creative activities stimulates the imagination, ignites inspiration, and cultivates a sense of curiosity and wonder. By embracing creativity in all forms, we can unleash our creative potential, discover hidden talents, and

enrich our lives with moments of beauty, wonder, and self-discovery.

3. **Therapeutic benefits of creative expression:** Creative expression offers many therapeutic benefits for our mental, emotional, and spiritual well-being. Here are some ways in which creative activities promote healing and self-discovery:

- **Stress reduction:** Creative pursuits such as painting, sculpting, drawing, dancing, playing music and writing require deep focus, allowing us to unwind, recharge, and find inner peace amidst life's challenges.

- **Emotional release:** Creative expression can provide a powerful means of emotional release. Through art, we can process complex emotions, confront inner conflicts, and find catharsis and closure.

- **Self-exploration:** Creativity invites us to explore our inner world, confront limiting beliefs, and embark on self-discovery and personal growth journeys. By expressing ourselves creatively, we gain insights into our values, desires, and aspirations, fostering greater self-awareness and self-acceptance.

- **Mindfulness and presence:** Engaging in creative activities promotes mindfulness and being fully present in the moment. They offer opportunities for flow states, where we lose ourselves in the creative process and may experience a profound sense of joy and fulfilment.

In conclusion, embracing creativity and expression enhances our lives with beauty, meaning, and purpose, enriching our journey of self-discovery, personal growth, and holistic well-being. By nurturing our creative spirit and exploring artistic outlets, we cultivate a deeper connection with ourselves and the world, fostering a life filled with inspiration, passion, and creative abundance.

Environmental wellness

Environmental wellness describes the relationship between us and our surroundings, highlighting the impact of environmental factors on our overall health and well-being. Here's an exploration of this vital dimension of wellness and practical suggestions for creating a nurturing and sustainable living space.

1. **Environmental factors and our overall health:** The environment in which we live, work, and play significantly influences our physical, mental, and emotional well-being. From the air we breathe to the spaces we live in, environmental factors play a crucial role in shaping our health outcomes and quality of life. Air quality, exposure to natural

light, access to green spaces, and proximity to pollutants can impact our breathing, immune systems, mood, cognitive performance, and stress levels. By cultivating a supportive and healthy environment, we can optimise our wellness and enhance our resilience to environmental stressors.

2. **Creating a nurturing and sustainable living space:** We cannot control the environment around us. However, we can all do some things to create a nurturing and sustainable living space to promote our health, harmony, and wider ecological balance. Here are some suggestions.

    - **Declutter:** Clearing clutter from our rooms, if needed, promotes well-being and mental clarity. Simplify your living space by removing unnecessary items, organising your belongings, and creating designated areas for different activities.

    - **Add greenery:** Introducing houseplants into your living space will not only add beauty and vibrancy but will also improve indoor air quality and enhance your overall well-being. Choose low-maintenance plants that thrive indoors and place them strategically throughout your home to purify the air and create a calming ambience.

Sparkle

- **Reduce exposure to toxins:** Avoid exposure to harmful chemicals and toxins by opting for natural, eco-friendly cleaning products, furnishings, and building materials. Choose non-toxic alternatives whenever possible and ventilate your living space regularly to improve air circulation and reduce indoor air pollution.

- **Create outdoor sanctuaries:** Cultivate outdoor sanctuaries, such as gardens, patios, or balconies, where you can connect with nature, relax, and recharge. Surround yourself with greenery, flowers, and natural elements to create tranquil and inviting outdoor spaces promoting relaxation, creativity, and connection with the natural world.

3. **Benefits of spending time in nature:** Spending time in nature and engaging in outdoor activities has many benefits for our physical, mental, and emotional well-being. Here's why connecting with nature is essential for environmental wellness.

    - **Stress reduction:** Immersing ourselves in natural environments, such as parks, forests, or beaches, helps reduce stress, lowers cortisol levels, and promotes relaxation and mental clarity.

- **Physical health:** Outdoor activities, such as hiking, biking, or gardening, maintain or improve our cardiovascular health, strength, and stamina.
- **Mood enhancement:** Exposure to natural light, fresh air, and scenic landscapes boosts our mood, uplifts our spirits, and enhances our happiness, contentment, and well-being.
- **Connection with the earth:** Connecting with nature fosters a sense of awe, reverence, and gratitude for the earth's beauty and biodiversity, deepening our appreciation for the interconnectedness of all living beings and ecosystems.

In conclusion, environmental wellness is essential for cultivating a healthy, balanced, and sustainable lifestyle. By creating nurturing living spaces, reducing environmental toxins, and immersing ourselves in nature, we can enhance our well-being, foster ecological stewardship, and contribute to a healthier planet for future generations.

Chapter 9
EPILOGUE – SPARKLING

Hello, sparklers!

As we end this journey together, I want to reflect on the incredible transformation and growth we've experienced. It's been quite a ride. From mastering the art of decision-making to nurturing meaningful relationships and embracing creativity, we've delved deep into the many facets of life that truly sparkle.

But here's the thing—our journey doesn't end here. It's just the beginning. As you embark on the next chapter of your life, I want you to carry the lessons you've learned like precious gems in your pocket, guiding your every step.

Remember the importance of self-care and nurturing your well-being inside and out. Whether making healthier food choices, prioritising quality sleep, or carving out time for creativity and self-expression, never underestimate the power of taking care of yourself.

Let's not forget the magic of relationships—those connections that light up our lives and bring us joy. Keep nurturing those bonds, communicating openly, and setting healthy boundaries. Your support network is your secret weapon, so cherish it and lean on it when necessary.

As you navigate life's ups and downs, remember to stay grounded in your values and beliefs. These guiding stars lead you toward your true north and help you stay true to yourself, no matter the challenges.

And finally, always remember that you have the power to choose how you live your life. Every decision, big or small, shapes your path and determines your destiny. So choose wisely, follow your heart, and never stop pursuing your dreams.

So here's to you, my fellow Sparklers – may your life sparkle and shine brighter. Keep embracing the journey, spreading love and light wherever you go, and never forget that the world is a more colourful place because you're in it.

With love and sparkles,

Nkechi

References

1. Covey, S. R. (2004). The 7 Habits of Highly Effective People: Powerful Lessons in Personal Change. Simon & Schuster.

2. Eze, J. (2020). Strong Walls, Stronger Gates: The Word of the LORD That Came to Jerry Eze, April 10, 2020. Kindle Edition.

3. Goleman, D. (2006). Emotional Intelligence: Why It Can Matter More Than IQ. Bantam.

4. Tracy, B. (2001). Eat That Frog!: 21 Great Ways to Stop Procrastinating and Get More Done in Less Time. Berrett-Koehler Publishers.

5. Vohs, K. D., & Baumeister, R. F. (Eds.). (2016). Handbook of Self-Regulation: Research, Theory, and Applications. Guilford Publications.

Printed in Great Britain
by Amazon